Ski Mountain

written by Kelly Gaffney

A trip to a ski mountain is lots of fun, but it can also be very cold.
Soft, white snow is all over the ground.
You can't see any grass at all.

Snow is on top of the trees.
It's also on top of the cars and buses.
You can see snow all around you
at a ski mountain.

Snow is made of water.
The snow on the ground
can be very soft.
Your feet go down as you walk.
You can't walk very quickly
across the snow at all.

At a ski mountain, people need
to bring lots of things.
They need a hat,
a coat and some gloves.
They also need skis,
boots and a helmet.
It can be very sunny on the snow.
So people have to take care
of their eyes, too.

9

There are lots of people
at a ski mountain.
Some people are skiing,
and some people are playing
in the snow.
Some children like
to make a snowman
from the soft, white snow.

You can ride on a chairlift
at a ski mountain.
A chairlift takes people
to the top of the hill.
You can see lots of things
from the chairlift.

People can go down the hill on skis.
People can go down the hill
on a snowboard, too.
Some of them go very fast.
Some of them go very slowly.
And some people fall over as they
go down the hill.

There are lots of fun things to do on a ski mountain.